Move It

PHYSICAL MOVEMENT AND LEARNING

ALISTAIR SMITH

Published by
Network Educational Press Ltd
PO Box 635
Stafford
ST16 1BF
www.networkpress.co.uk

Reprinted 2003
© Alistair Smith 2002

ISBN 1 85539 123 6

Layout Design: Neil Hawkins – NEP
Illustrations: Oliver Caviglioli

Printed in Great Britain by
MPG Books Ltd., Bodmin, Cornwall.

Contents

Introduction

One summer's evening I found myself outside a street café in Ronda in Southern Spain. It was late evening and the noise of the café filled the street. Two young girls, one aged about ten and the other about seven, were playing by the tables nearby. The older and taller girl clapped a rhythm with her hands and the younger girl was encouraged to follow. Then the older girl clapped with her hands and stamped with her feet. The younger girl was encouraged to follow. After much trial and error, both clapped and stamped in unison. They were completely engaged in what they were doing, oblivious to other children and other games, to motor cycles, to dogs barking and to their parent's entreaties to sit down. There is no better way to learn and to enjoy the experience as you do so, than through physical movement. This book is an introduction to physical movement and learning.

Throughout this book you will come across the term 'brain break'. I use this term to describe a physical activity which is deliberate, involves slow and considered movement and which requires thought. I am of the view that planned physical movements can support a child's learning. This book gives you a series of exercises and physical movements to help your child improve his or her capacity, willingness and readiness to learn. The exercises can all be completed at home or in a classroom.

There is a great deal of accumulated research evidence – of varying quality – in support of physical exercise and physical reprieve to complement academic learning. However, the academic research evidence which attempts to link specific physical exercises to specific academic improvements is not so compelling. This is mostly because of poor controls, lack of focus and difficulty of isolating contributory factors. Despite this, many teachers and parents do offer anecdotal evidence of learning improvements in the children with whom they have worked. Maybe that is enough? What we offer in this book is a series of exercises and activities for a number of purposes that relate to learning. The exercises provide opportunities for physical reprieve, they can link to learning, they can contribute to improvements in motor control and are fun and memorable in themselves. There is good evidence from around the world of the value of distributed rehearsal. That is, less content and more opportunity to go over and review the content at spaced intervals. Space the use of these exercises out. Use them a little and often to complement learning over time.

It is important for children to understand that the lifestyle they lead always has some choice built into it. Their physical and intellectual health will be shaped by the choices they make about eating, drinking, exercise, sleep, play, what they watch on TV and the computer games they play. I include a short summary of lifestyle research for teachers and parents in Section Two. In Section Three there is a Taxonomy of Brain Breaks which describes how each type of activity has been selected and designed and how they all relate to each other. Section Three also contains some health and safety advice.

The exercises are listed by type in Section Four. Section Five contains ideas for resources and for further reading.

The state of being immersed in an activity which, by its very nature, is so absorbing that time seems to stand still, is sometimes referred to as 'flow'. Flow is sometimes achieved by top athletes when they are performing at the highest level, by elderly gardeners who have to be called indoors because it has begun to be too dark to see their flowers, and by young children who clap and stamp out games in the street. I hope that you, your children and your pupils enjoy the learning exercises you find in this book.

Alistair Smith
July 2002

The significance of movement to learning

MOVE IT is a book of practical physical movements to aid learning. The proposition is that physical movement can offer reprieve, it can link to learning, it can improve motor control and it can be fun and memorable in itself.

Here are ten arguments for adding movement to learning:

1 Movement is an integral part of human development.

2 Mimicry, a form of controlled movement, is the most natural form of human learning.

3 The more we do it, the better we become at it. Oxygen uptake becomes more efficient, little and large motor control is improved.

4 Procedural learning sticks. When something is learned through physical movement it doesn't dislodge easily.

5 Multiple learning systems are actively engaged. Rehearse in different ways and the learning is deeper.

6 Adds value to one's life. Being physically healthy, having good co-ordination and balance helps you cope better with different everyday challenges.

7 Highly valued. Physical skills such as those used in silversmithing, carpentry, dentistry, construction, sports such as tennis and golf and even the high wire act have financial value.

8 Integrity of method. Whilst semantic and episodic memory is vulnerable with ageing and illness, procedural memory is less so.

9 Transferable. Physical learning is carried with you and into all situations.

10 Independent of other measures of intelligence. Physical learners seem to have a high capacity for adapting and learning new skills.

MOVE IT is a book with a long history of research behind it. If you wish to find out more about the links between child development, the architecture of the human brain and the development of motor skills you should read *The Brain's Behind It*. This book is an attempt to explain in simple terms what research tells us about the brain and learning.

Ten physical functions enhanced by movement in learning:

1 Synaptic connections. Through physical engagement with the surrounding world connections between brain cells are laid down. This happens in sensitive periods which begin at birth. Encourage young children to stretch, play, make physical contact, walk, throw, catch, run, swim and climb from the earliest!

2 Motor control. The development of what, in this book, I call little and large motor control, co-ordination of voluntary movement, begins to decline in the brain from around age 13 to 15 when about 50 per cent of the brain tissue that controls motor skills are pruned away. Thus, activities that require motor skills, such as playing an instrument or a sport, may also have a critical period during childhood in which it is easiest to acquire the necessary abilities.

3 Brain integration. The corpus callosum – 200 million nerve fibres going across a structure 10 cm long and 2.5 cm high – completes its maturation in the late adolescent years. The corpus callosum acts like a relay station sending electrical signals between the two hemispheres of the cortex. Its successful development and integration is part of the wiring up of the adolescent brain. It is not considered to be fully integrated until the age range 16 through to about 25.

4 Balance and movement. The cerebellum plays a leading role in movement and learning. As the child practises crawling, the large motor movements are rehearsed, adjusted, repeated and improved. Adjustments become littler and littler, the movements quicker and more precise. Children who have the slightest damage to the cerebellum do not make this same steady progress. Impairments in the cerebellum can lead to difficulties in co-ordinating movement, catching a ball, tapping out a rhythm, balancing on a beam, skipping and playing a percussion instrument.

5 Attention and reward. Attention is directed by curiosity. Physical movement, changes in shape and pattern, noise and light along with any contrast, engages curiosity. Neurotransmitters, such as dopamine, are associated with a pleasure response and are activated by physical activity and by novelty. Learning which contains these elements has a motivation and reward dimension of its own.

6 Circulation and respiration. Getting more oxygen up into the brain and doing so more regularly helps our learning. A five year old uses nearly 50 per cent of the oxygen in the body to keep the brain alert and engaged. Try teaching a class of 30 five year-olds in a hot and stuffy room and you will see the point.

7 Stress. Physical reprieve goes some way to relieving stress. When stressed, children lapse into any combination of aggression, avoidance, apprehension or over-attachment. What we sometimes call the four 'f's': fight, flight, freeze and flock. Robust physical movement can decrease the likelihood of this happening.

8 Sensory motor systems. Our bodies are highly specialized problem seeking and solving machines. We contain sophisticated communications systems so that thought can be quickly translated into action. Highly interconnected, the systems nevertheless need practice to become even more efficient. The short cut to doing this is physical activity. For example, there is good evidence that practising eye tracking movements can help some children with their reading difficulties.

9 Cognition. There is good evidence to support the idea of a healthy mind in a healthy body. UK schools' researchers found a link between regular exercise and improvements in academic performance. More than 1,400 children took part in the research. Regular exercise at least three or four times a week seemed to make a difference in the classroom. Others found that pupils with a high participation in sports tend to have lower truancy rates and less bad behaviour. Being able to represent conceptual ideas, emotions and relationships through physical movement is high art.

10 Memory. If you want something to be remembered get it in the muscle! Facts, figures, events, people and places utilize semantic and episodic memory systems whereas physical interpretation and rehearsal accesses a completely different – procedural – system. Muscle memory offers a fast route to recall.

If young children had been intended to sit still for long periods of time then they would have been born with Velcro on their bottoms! Get them up. MOVE IT and learn!

Lifestyle choice

Some recent research suggests that one in five adults in the UK are obese. More and more children are susceptible to the illnesses historically associated with a sedentary lifestyle and they are slowing down younger. A child's lifestyle impacts on its ability and willingness to learn. Physical exercise and diet play their part in shaping the brain they inherit as adults. Proper nutrition, hydration, sleep and exercise are all important. Children need to understand that they have lifestyle choices and that how they exercise these choices will help shape their success in life

How high a child flies in life depends upon the start, they are given, the support they receive and the three 'A's'. The three 'A' formula looks like this:

$$\text{Altitude} = \text{Aptitude} \times \text{Attitude} \times \text{Activation}$$

Help is needed along the way. But how you fly can be seen as a function of aptitude times attitude times activation. In other words, it's no use having talents if the commitment to utilize the talents isn't there, and it's no use having talents and commitment unless as a result of this something happens.

A teacher cannot control all three 'A's', but the teacher can bring direct influence. The teacher can also help children and, to a lesser extent, parents understand which lifestyle choices have a bearing on learning success. Here are a few.

Inherited factors

An unborn child is already beginning to inherit its mother's lifestyle. A mother who experiments with drugs, who smokes throughout pregnancy, who drinks alcohol to excess risks catastrophic consequences for her baby's brain. Poor diet, exposure to toxins and radiation, high sustained anxiety and illness can all have a damaging effect on the unborn child's subsequent health.

Nutrition

A child who has had no breakfast or an inappropriate breakfast is more likely to underperform. We all have different metabolic systems. Some of us are morning people and some of us night people but if, over a sustained period of time, our system runs down because of insufficient fuel, learning suffers.

A British study has found that one in four schoolgirls of secondary age studied are damaging their IQs by dieting and depriving themselves of iron. A very small drop in iron levels caused a fall in IQ. Researchers found that there was a highly significant difference in IQ between iron-deficient anaemic girls, with the lowest levels of iron in their blood, iron-deficient and iron-replete girls.

In a further study by nutritionists of 6,000 adolescent boys and girls those with insufficient iron in their diets were more than twice as likely to score below average in mathematics tests. Boys and girls with higher levels of iron scored ten per cent higher in the maths tests.

Skipping breakfast leads to poorer academic performance. In a process known as metabolic starvation, focused attention, recall and coping with complex mental tasks becomes increasingly more difficult.

Hydration

Being properly hydrated brings obvious benefits. All round health is improved, concentration times extend, we become more resistant to illness, our ability to remember is improved. Most of us are properly hydrated through the food and drink we regularly consume. Here are some relevant facts about the importance of water:

- The brain is 75 per cent water.
- Blood is 92 per cent water.
- Bones are 22 per cent water.
- Muscles are 75 per cent water.
- Water carries nutrients and oxygen to all cells in the body.
- Dehydration can cause headaches and dizziness.
- Water regulates body temperature.
- Water protects and cushions vital organs.
- Water helps to convert food into energy.
- Water cushions the joints.

Children who are dehydrated are not in a good state for learning. Fizzy drinks, drinks laced with chemicals and drinks with an excess of sugar do not necessarily help children learn better. Being properly hydrated does help children learn better.

Sleep

Sleep of the right sort helps learning. The best learning occurs when two types of sleep – REM and slow-wave – take place during the course of the night. A good sleep is important after learning because it is during sleep with oscillations between REM and slow-wave in roughly 90-minute cycles that consolidation of what happened and when occurs.

Cheat on sleep for only a few nights and you increase brain levels of the stress chemical cortisol. About two-thirds of the population fail to get enough sleep. With very young children lack of sufficient uninterrupted sleep causes behaviour problems. A study of 500 children under five years of age found that those who slept less than ten hours a day, including naps, were 25 per cent more likely to misbehave. They would throw temper tantrums, act aggressively to others, be more vocal in their attention seeking and more demanding of adult attention. Children who slept 12 or more hours a day were much less likely to behave in this way.

Energy levels

Humans have highs and lows for energy and for intellectual functions. These ups and downs are called circadian rhythms and they apply to many of our bodily functions. A circadian rhythm is basically a 24-hour cycle. Our highs and lows occur at 90–110 minute intervals. Some also argue that these shifts coincide with highs or lows in terms of hemispheric activity. In a classroom at any one point some children will be on an energy high while others are on a low point, some will have more activity in the left of the brain while others have more in the right. There is no accurate way of predicting this! However, another theory suggests that cross-lateral activity can compensate for this temporary shift in dominance. In other words, to regulate energy and activity levels in a class, build in lateralizers every 90–110 minutes.

Oxygenation

One benefit of frequent structured physical reprieve is the release of more oxygen up into the brain. Simply by standing up this process begins. Stooping and sitting are the two postures which most aggravate back pain. Stasis fatigue – stuck for too long sitting – is real. When you get children up and out of their seats you advantage their learning.

Laughter

Research on laughter and learning points to improved learning gains when intellectual challenges are preceded and reprieved by laughter. When a child is laughing he or she is not likely to be anxious. When anxiety is reduced, you will take more risks. When you take more risks the likelihood of real learning goes up. Laughter improves your immunity to disease, it releases natural neural growth factors and it increases the bonds within the group.

The best learning environments are environments which encourage risk taking, which utilize mimicry, imagination, creativity and play. Such environments also encourage reflection on all the variables which influence learning.

Brain breaks — a taxonomy

MOVE IT is organized so that you can easily use and adapt each brain break. We call them brain breaks because we believe that they provide an alternative means of fully engaging the brain. Brain breaks are best used to complement learning. They can be used before, during or after formal learning and, indeed, can be part of helping the child understand and recall concepts and content.

In order to use the brain breaks you should try them yourself first. You should also check your class medical history to ensure that children are not prohibited from physical activities. Make a professional judgment about how to progress through the exercises.

Use **Relaxers** to help children understand the difference between feeling anxious and feeling calm. For most learning situations calm is better! Many children do not, however, experience anything other than anxiety in their lives. Relaxers should be practised in a slow, methodical and considered way. Eventually children should be able to use the Relaxers as and when they need to calm themselves down.

Energizers have the opposite effect to Relaxers and should be used sparingly! Deliberately fun and exploratory, Energizers usually involve pairs or teams, often have a comic and creative element and lift the energy levels of the children. The typical time for an Energizer would be mid afternoon when tiredness is creeping in. The typical circumstance would be in a hot and stuffy environment. The typical benefit would be an instant rejuvenation of energy levels and spirits!

Stretchers help children develop physical flexibility. Stretchers help children name body parts and understand how to use – and look after – their bodies. Take care with Stretchers. Children are all at different stages of physical development and have different vulnerabilities. Move through each stage of the exercise slowly, demonstrating good posture and balance as you go.

Lateralizers help children understand left and right. Lateralizers develop co-ordination, integration and balance. Crawling, reaching out with alternative grasping hands, swimming, throwing and intercepting are all naturally lateralized activities. Some children miss out or do not fully rehearse such movements at crucial stages in their young lives. Some of us heavily favour one side of our bodies. Good sensory integration comes about with health and with regular opportunity to develop left-right co-ordination of large and little movements. To work at their best Lateralizers need to be considered rather than impulsive, slow rather than quick, smooth rather than jerky, controlled rather than unco-ordinated. A range of good Lateralizers should be part of your teaching repertoire.

Brain breaks for **Little n' Large** Movement improve hand eye co-ordination and voluntary motor control. Brain Breaks for Little n' Large Movement also help children perfect controlled movements which will be needed in a learning environment. Managing and controlling a pen is not easy. Freehand drawing is not easy. Manipulating oneself in and out of and around desks and tables safely is not easy. Holding the book and turning the pages is not easy. Brain breaks for Little n' Large Movement rehearse such movements in a non-threatening and safe way.

Co-ordinates involve working with a partner in a structured way, Co-ordinates combine any of the above brain breaks depending on the learning purpose. With the introduction of a partner, the opportunities to become excitable increase! Arrive at Co-ordinates after children become familiar with the basic brain break exercises and routines. Emphasize smooth controlled and voluntary movement at all times. Encourage children to observe, mentally rehearse what they are going to do and then do the movements.

With the introduction of **Linkers** we begin to experience how physical movement links to improving learning skills and to understanding and remembering content. Be aware that children pass through a developmental stage where abstract representation is beyond them into a stage where it begins to be easier. A good example is the number line. At what point in a child's development does a row of one's friends become a series of numbers? Is it potentially confusing for the teacher to describe the symbols for numbers in the book with the same words as she describes my friends standing up in a row? Potentially yes, it is confusing. However, part of the professional repertoire of the skilled practitioner is to be able to select the appropriate intervention at the appropriate stage. What MOVE IT provides are more interventions. With Linkers there need never be dead learning time in your school day. Use Linkers when children are waiting in assembly, queuing for lunch, waiting in line after break. Linkers are simple brain breaks which allow children to rehearse their learning at any time.

The last type of brain break we offer are **Eye Trackers**. A very high percentage of reading problems in UK schoolchildren can be traced to poor eye tracking or what is sometimes known as 'eye wobble'. Eye Trackers help the child improve eye control. If a child has eye wobble then professional help is needed and should be sought. Eye Trackers are no substitute but can be a useful, immediate and fun way to help all children develop their ability to focus and track.

In MOVE IT the following terms are used and you should be familiar with them:

brief	where we explain the purposes and the benefits of the movements before we begin to use them
lateral	means to the outside, left or right
handpen	hands clasped together to form a pen
freeze n' flow	pause, stay still, then move
slomo	slow movements

stickies	these are the moments when the child struggles and finds it difficult. Stickies are good for learning. Unless you struggle how will you get better? Watch out for the sticky moments. Debrief on the stickies
free expression	where children choose their own brain breaks and, until the teacher says otherwise, practise at their own speed
de-brief	when we discuss and agree what we have learned at the end of a brain break session

Before you begin explain the what and the how. Say what you are going to do and why – sell the benefits and say how you will do it. Let children understand the broad purposes and the principles so they can adapt for themselves and build in debriefing: what was good? What did you notice? What did you do well? What will you do better? How should we improve? What other ideas can we try next time?

Have fun!

Safety first

The brain breaks described in this book do not offer an alternative to therapeutic or remedial interventions prescribed by health professionals. Nor is what is described a complementary therapy. Nor will these exercises ever replace or supplant the work of a good classroom teacher. Nor will they alone cure dyslexia or dyspraxia or make your child more academic. However, we do hope that they will add to the repertoire of the caring parent and complement the work of the teacher while being enjoyable into the bargain.

With exercises which involve unusual postures or stretching, check before starting that there are no recorded health issues with any of the children. Warm up by starting slowly and explaining the safest way to do so as you go. Make sure clothing is not too tight or restrictive. Work in safe, dry and warm places. Enjoy the brain breaks!

The brain-break exercises

Relaxers

The Principle

Relaxers help children experience the difference between feeling relaxed and feeling anxious or stressed.

Teaching Tips

1 Take your time...

2 Start with breathing patterns...

3 Practise relaxation from the top down...

Benefits to Children

1 An appreciation of the difference between tense and relaxed states.

2 Understanding simple techniques to help become more relaxed.

3 Knowing names for different parts of the body.

Scuba

Practise good breathing – deep and slow. Count in and count out. Don't hold your breath, just breath deeply…

Scuba Tens

Practise good breathing for ten breaths – deep and slow. Count in and count out. Don't hold your breath, just breath deeply…

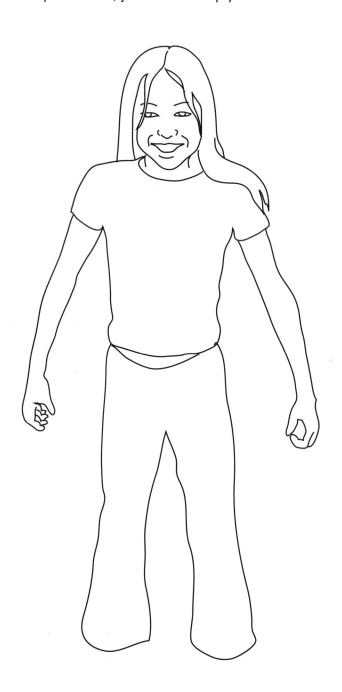

Shampoo

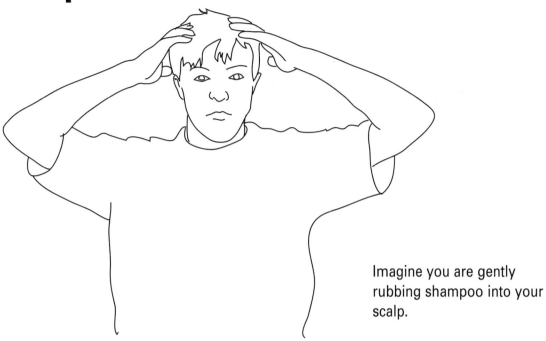

Imagine you are gently rubbing shampoo into your scalp.

Big Yawn

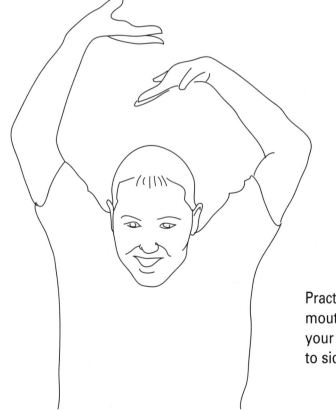

Practise yawning! Stretch your mouth as wide as you can. Stick your chin out and move it from side to side.

Noddies

Practise nodding your head slowly forwards and back. Do it really slowly and carefully. Breathe slowly and gently as you go. Now do it from side to side. See how carefully you can do it!

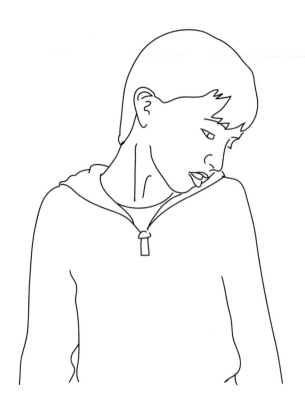

Ears

Hold your ears and slowly roll your ear lobes between finger and thumb.

Hold your ears with your opposite hand and slowly roll your ear lobes between finger and thumb.

Eyes

Practise rolling your eyes in circles one way slowly, then the other way slowly.

Now close your eyelids and try it again.

Centre Up

Place the tips of your thumbs against the bones at the top of your chest and just under your neck. Feel around till you find a little hollow. Now push gently but firmly in then up. Do it several times.

Now close your eyes and do it.

Chopsticks

On a partner's back do gentle chops with the back of your hand. Do them across your partner's back but do it gently.

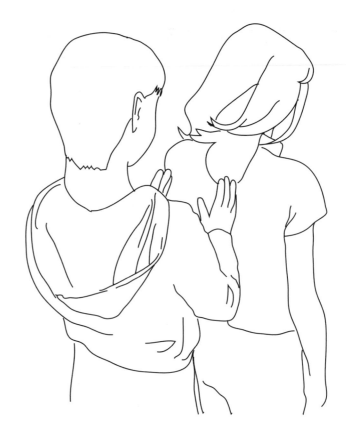

Squeegees

On a partner's back do gentle squeezes with your fingers. Do it across your partner's back but do it gently.

Soccer Massage

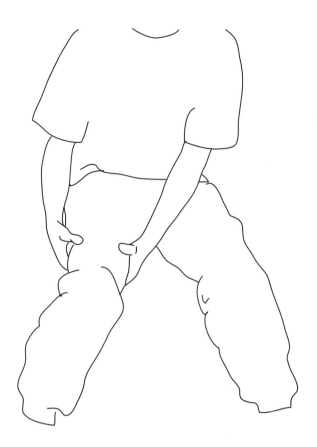

Place your hands behind
your thighs and gently
squeeze. Move up and
down squeezing as you go.

Now do the same with
your calves

Toes Up

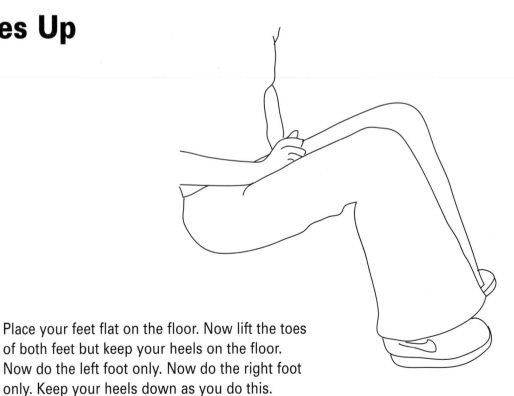

Place your feet flat on the floor. Now lift the toes
of both feet but keep your heels on the floor.
Now do the left foot only. Now do the right foot
only. Keep your heels down as you do this.

The brain-break exercises

Energizers

The Principle

Energizers help children become more physically alert. Energisers improve oxygen uptake and can be used to help children remain attentive.

Teaching Tips

1 Use a calm voice when issuing instructions (they will not be calm)...

2 Always use starting rituals which encourage good posture, good listening and responsibility.

3 Safety first: remind children to stick to the rules...

Benefits to Children

1 Provides a reprieve from stasis fatigue!

2 Can help refocus energies towards academic work.

3 Creates a sense of anticipation and so can be used as part of a reward system.

Clappit

Follow a partner or a group leader who claps a rhythm. As they clap you wait a second and then copy them. Try and get exactly the same sound each time. When you get really good you can clap your hands and then stamp your feet!

Clappit n' Snappit

Follow a partner or a group leader who claps a rhythm and snaps their fingers too!

23

Tickle Me!

Try tickling yourself!
Does it work?
Try different places.

Tummy Slapper

On your tummy do gentle
slaps with the flat palm of
your hand.

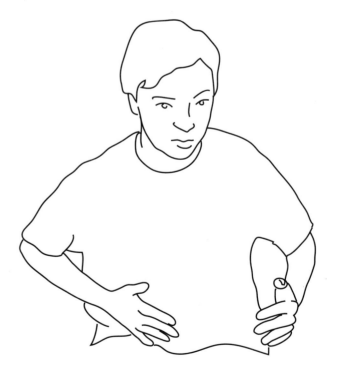

Boogie Band

When the music plays use your imaginary instrument to play along.

People Hunt

Find someone who... Find three people who...

The brain-break exercises

Stretchers

The Principle

Stretchers help children improve posture, balance, flexibility of muscles and joints and awareness of their bodies.

Teaching Tips

1 Get warm first: avoid draughty places or cold rooms...

2 Get relaxed first, keep your voice calm and slow, use the breathing techniques...

3 Demonstrate each exercise first and do them slowly...

Benefits to Children

1 Improves posture, balance, flexibility of muscles and joints.

2 Helps respiratory and circulation systems.

3 Children can practise these activities at any time.

Tall Poppies

Stand up and, keeping your feet stuck to the floor, sway gently in the wind like tall poppies growing up to the sun. Sway left and right gently, now back and forward, back and forward. Stretch up to the Sun.

Hair Piece

See if you can get your hair to move without touching or shaking it!

PS. Here's a secret tip. Move your hair by trying to wrinkle your head!

27

Shoulder Shrugs

Practise shrugging your shoulders forward slowly, then backwards slowly.

Doing the Rounds

With your elbows at shoulder height practice making big circles, then small circles, forwards and backwards.

Flat Feet

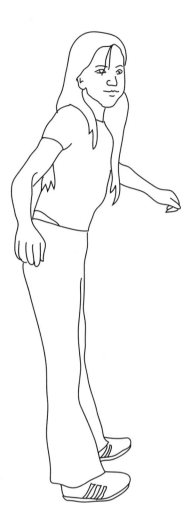

Practise placing your feet flat on the floor, now gently rock onto your heels, now back onto your toes.

Circle Toes

Sitting in your seat with your hands holding the seat, extend your feet forwards and rotate your feet together one way then the other.

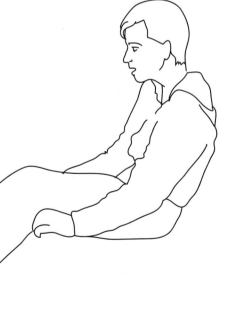

29

More Circle Toes

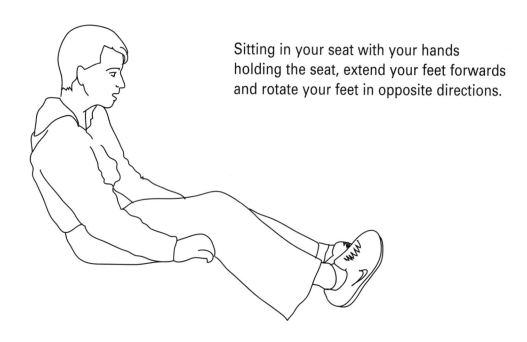

Sitting in your seat with your hands holding the seat, extend your feet forwards and rotate your feet in opposite directions.

Simple Stretch

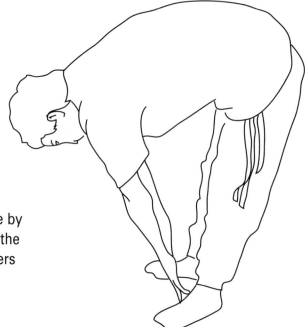

Stand up tall and in a space by yourself. Bend gently from the waist and stretch your fingers towards your toes.

Simple Stretch

Stand up tall and in a space by yourself. Place one foot out in front and flat on the floor, slide the other foot back with just your toes touching. Bend gently at the knee and stretch carefully.

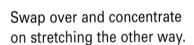
Swap over and concentrate on stretching the other way.

Place your right hand above your head and then slowly take it down your back as far as it will comfortably go. Now with your left hand hold your right elbow gently.

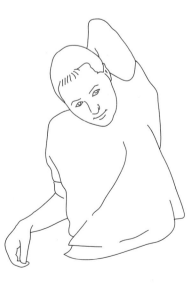

Swap hands and try again.

The brain-break exercises

Lateralizers

The Principle

Lateralizers involve crossing the mid line of the body – 'from nose to toes' – with smooth, co-ordinated movement. Lateralizers help children understand left and right. They help develop lateral co-ordination, bodily integration and voluntary motor control. Lateralisers are an essential part of your brain break repertoire.

Teaching Tips

1 Ensure children have sufficient space to move around...

2 Start easy and slow, demonstrating the mid-line principle as you go...

3 Encourage as you go and persist: many children will find these difficult ...

Benefits to Children

1 Improves understanding of left and right.

2 Helps with large and little motor control, hand and eye co-ordination.

3 Integrates brain function related to voluntary movement.

4 Improves self-esteem.

Pear Tree Picker

Hands stretched out high above your head pick imaginary pears, alternately left and right. Now pick lemons, they are lower down. Now pick strawberries, they are on the ground. Now try pear, apple, strawberry. How about strawberry, apple, pear?

Swimmer

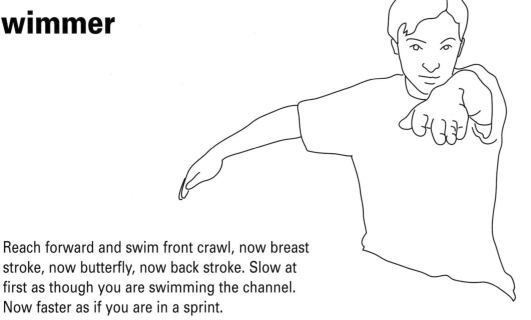

Reach forward and swim front crawl, now breast stroke, now butterfly, now back stroke. Slow at first as though you are swimming the channel. Now faster as if you are in a sprint.

Cross Crawler

Morecambe and Wise

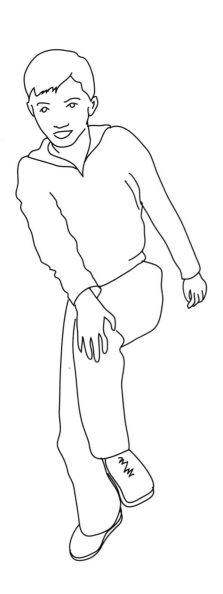

With your right hand touch your left knee. Now with your left hand touch your right knee. Do it slowly and with big movements. Bring you knee up to meet your hand. Now try it with your elbows to your knees.

With your right hand go around your back and touch your left heel. Now with your left hand go around your back and touch your right heel. Do it slowly and with big movements. Bring your heel up to meet your hand. Now try alternate Cross Crawler with Morecambe and Wise.

Super Swapper

With your right thumb and forefinger pinch your nose, with your left thumb and forefinger hold your right ear. Now swap and swap again.

Circle Time

Touch your forefingers together out from the front of your face. Touch the tips of the outstretched fingers together. Now rotate in a circle but in opposite directions. When you get really good at circles try and do squares, then rectangles and how about a figure 8?

Windmills

Try the same thing with your arms! Rotate them at the same time in wide circles from the shoulder but in opposite directions.

Alphabet Soup

Look at the large picture the teacher has put up for the class. Use the alphabet and say it out loud as you do the movements – right hand, left hand or together.

Alphabet Duck Soup

Use the alphabet and say it out loud as you
do the movements – right hand, left hand,
two hands together or duck.

Alphabet Double Duck Soup

Use the alphabet and say it out loud as you
do the movements – right hand, left hand,
two hands together or double duck.

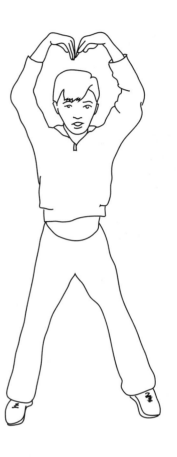

Alphabet Animal Soup

Use the alphabet and say it out
loud as you do the movements –
right hand, left hand, two hands
together or an animal movement
told to you by your teacher.

The brain-break exercises

Large

The Principle

Brain breaks for Large Movement focus on the steady manipulation of the large limbs. Essential movements are stretching, lifting and lowering, pushing and pulling, and balancing.

Teaching Tips

1 Ensure children have sufficient space to move around...

2 Start easy and slow, progress to increasingly more demanding brain breaks...

3 Encourage as you go and persist: many children will find these difficult ...

Benefits to Children

1 Improves balance.

2 Helps with large motor control, co-ordination and flexibility.

3 Integrates brain function related to voluntary movement.

Tiny Chi

Slow patterned movements Tai Chi style. The teacher models and the class follows. Nice and slow and steady, breathing evenly and regularly as you go.

Armworks

Both arms outstretched on either side. Now do circles. Start with forwards motion, then back. Do big slow circles. Now try squares. Now try circling forwards with one arm and backwards with the other. Swap over. Now try squares forwards and back. When you have practised, do it with your eyes closed.

39

Legworks

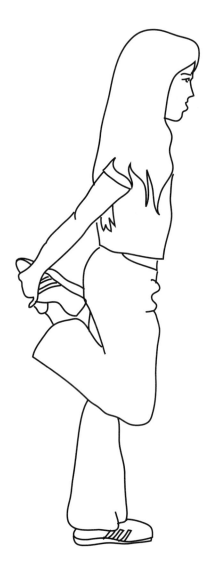

Feet placed slightly apart and flat on the ground. Pick up your right foot with your right hand and lift gently to the back. Now back down. Do the same with your left.

Now try lifting your right leg up and into your chest. Hold your knee with your right hand. Now back down. Do the same with your left. When you have practised, do it with your eyes closed. Take care!

Foothold

Balance a bean bag or koosh ball on the top of your foot and hold it above the ground. Keep it still and in place as you count to ten.

Balance a bean bag or koosh ball on the top of your foot and hold it above the ground. Keep it still and in place as you say the alphabet.

Balance a bean bag or koosh ball on the top of your foot and hold it above the ground. Keep it still and in place as you say the alphabet backwards.

Do the above but with the bean bag or koosh ball on the other foot.

Put your hand on your back. Now give yourself a big pat and say 'well done'.

The brain-break exercises

Little

The Principle

Brain breaks for Little Movement focus on dexterity of the fingers and thumbs. This helps children when they have to quickly become adept at manipulating objects such as pens, pencils and brushes.

Teaching Tips

1 Ensure children are sitting comfortably...

2 Do the warm ups first...

3 Adapt and improve...

Benefits to children

1 Helps improve handwriting.

2 Develops flexibility and strength in fingers.

3 Improves confidence and ability to manipulate objects with close control.

Warm Ups

Play an imaginary piano.
Play with both hands and all
fingers.

Hold an imaginary butterfly
between finger and thumb. Pass
it to your other hand and then
back and forth gently – it is a
butterfly – until each finger has
touched the butterfly.

With your right hand touch each
finger to your thumb one at a
time. Touch once. Now do the
left. Now same again, but this
time touch twice.

43

Warm Ups (cont)

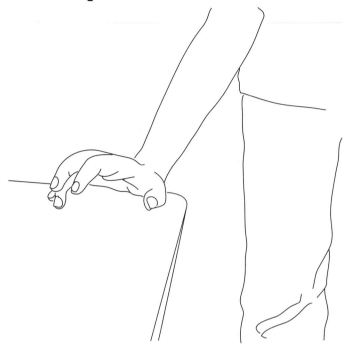

Drum your fingers on the edge of the desk so it makes a quiet drumming sound. Try and make a sound with each finger as it touches. Keep your hand close to the desk top and as still as possible and just move the fingers.

Steeples

Make a steeple with your fingers in front of your face, now lift each pair of fingers together starting with your index fingers. Keep your lips and teeth together.

Make a steeple with your fingers in front of your face, now lift each pair of fingers together starting with your index fingers. Count quietly aloud as you do so.

Rounds

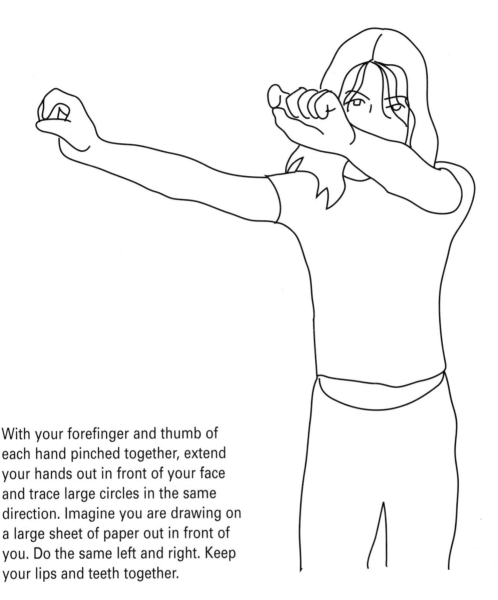

With your forefinger and thumb of each hand pinched together, extend your hands out in front of your face and trace large circles in the same direction. Imagine you are drawing on a large sheet of paper out in front of you. Do the same left and right. Keep your lips and teeth together.

With your forefinger and thumb of each hand pinched together, extend your hands out in front of your face and trace large circles in the opposite direction. Keep your lips and teeth together.

Now do the above, but on the surface of the desk.

The brain-break exercises

Co-ordinates

The Principle

Co-ordinates involve working with a partner in a structured way. Co-ordinates develops observation, language exchange, co-operation and self-awareness. It build a further dimension into brain break activity and so forms a natural extension to what goes before.

Teaching Tips

1 Choose pairs for physical as well as behavioural match up...

2 Build on what has gone before: do not introduce Co-ordinates without first having done Relaxers and basic brain breaks...

3 De-briefing is a must! Build in a debrief: What was good? What did you notice? What did you do well? What will you do better next time?

Benefits to Children

1 Helps improve behaviour.

2 Significant improvements in physical co-ordination and dexterity.

3 Improves social skills, confidence, trust and self-esteem.

Mirror Me

More Mirror Me

Face your partner. Observe the movements your partner makes, now begin to slowly copy the same movements. Do it slowly and carefully and try and get everything right.

Stand facing your partner. Observe the movements your partner makes, now begin to slowly copy the same movements. Do it slowly and carefully and try and get everything right.

Mirror More than Me

Sit back to back. Listen as your partner breathes slowly and deeply, now begin to slowly copy the same pattern. Do it slowly and carefully and try and get everything right.

Mirror More than Me 2

Sit back to back. Listen as your partner talks quietly, now begin to slowly copy her voice. Do it carefully and try and get everything right. Listen to the sounds carefully. Listen for high or low, fast or slow, sounds going up or down, sentences beginning and ending.

Shoulder2Shoulder

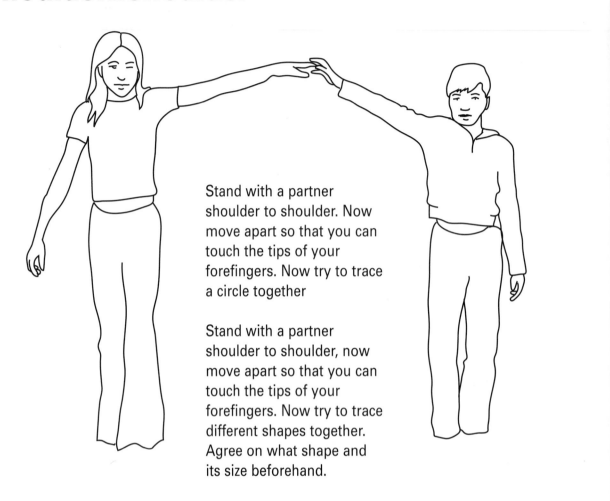

Stand with a partner shoulder to shoulder. Now move apart so that you can touch the tips of your forefingers. Now try to trace a circle together

Stand with a partner shoulder to shoulder, now move apart so that you can touch the tips of your forefingers. Now try to trace different shapes together. Agree on what shape and its size beforehand.

Desk Doubles

With a partner sit either side of a desk. Your partner should place both hands flat on the desk. With your finger and thumb 'draw' round the shape of their hands. Do it three times forwards and back, then swap.

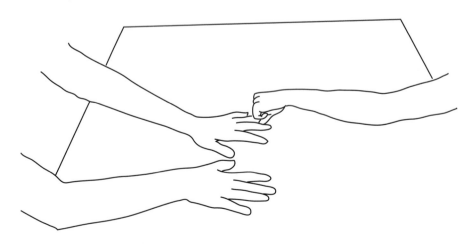

With a partner sit either side of a desk. Your partner should place both hands flat on the desk and so should you. Take turns to lift different fingers without taking any other fingers off the desk. The partner has five seconds to lift exactly the same finger from the same hand.

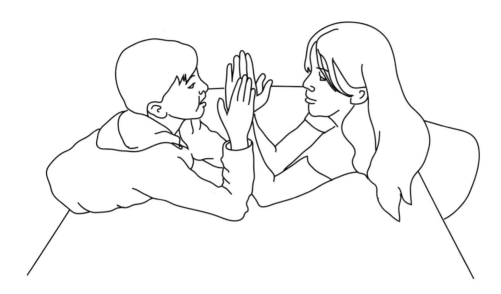

With a partner sit either side of a desk. Place your elbows on the desk against your partners. Your partner places his hands either side of yours with open palms. You have to push your hands out without moving your elbows.

Swap with your partner and now try again.

With a partner sit either side of a desk. Hold hands over the middle of the desk. Slowly begin to 'saw logs' by moving your hands back and forward over the desk. Gradually get faster.

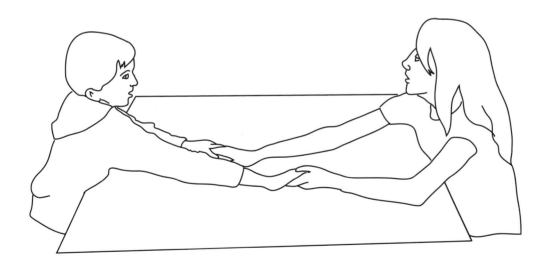

Finger Aerobics

Do finger aerobics! With a partner sit alongside each other or either side of a desk. Your partner should place both hands flat on the desk and so should you. Take turns to lift different fingers without taking any other fingers off the desk.

Do it together and in sequence. Start with simple lifts with each finger in turn, then do taps, then go for bends, the big stretches!

Chair Pair

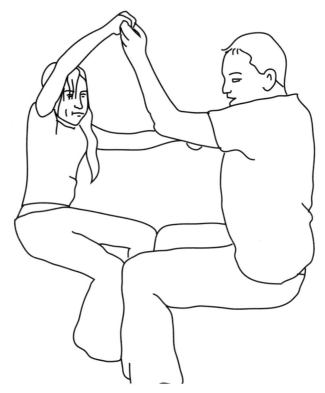

With a partner sit on chairs facing each other with your knees and toes touching. Hold hands over the middle. Slowly try these actions: raising a flag, swatting a fly, serving at a tennis match, driving a bus with a large steering wheel, boxing, picking up a very delicate flower. Hold hands all the time. Stay seated.

Chair Pair (cont)

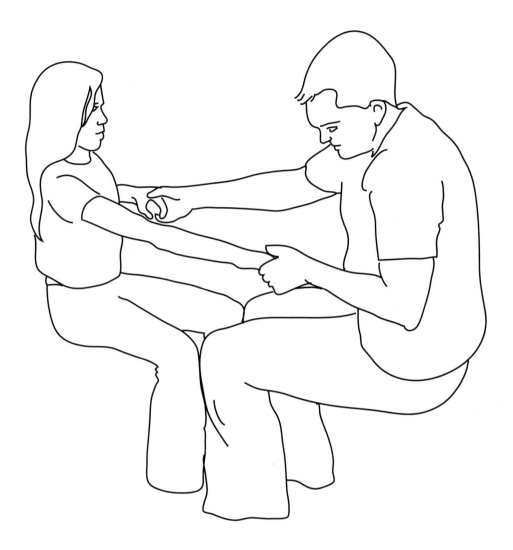

With a partner sit on chairs facing each other with your knees and toes touching. Hold hands over the middle. Slowly begin to 'saw logs' by moving your hands back and forward. Stay seated. Gradually get faster.

The brain-break exercises

Linkers

The Principle

Linkers are the most radical MOVE IT approach to learning. Brain breaks are deliberately used to communicate content in a memorable and distinctive way. Most of the exercises need a larger space in which to work. The sample below gives a sense of what is possible.

Teaching Tips

1 Use the brain-break activity to demonstrate or to complement or to rehearse essential learning and not as a substitute activity. Timelines in history, for example, can and should be represented in a number of ways.

2 Make the learning connections explicit as you go; encourage children to do the same.

3 Debriefing, once again, is vital.

Benefits to Children

1 Helps them stay engaged with learning while alleviating physical fatigue.

2 Is highly memorable and distinctive.

3 Demonstrates that learning occurs other than in paper and pencil experiences.

Art and Design

Touch and Go

Find five things made of wood and touch them, now four things made of wool and touch them, now three things made of paper and touch them, now two things made of plastic and touch them, now find one thing made of skin and touch it!

Sculpture

In your group organize yourselves into a body sculpture to represent one of these ideas: trust, courage, wealth, honesty, fame.

Self-Portrait

An artist is going to draw you. Put yourself in your favourite pose and we will see if we can guess what you have chosen and why.

Body Machinery

In your group organize yourselves into a body sculpture to represent people in action. Try these first, then choose your own: football crowd, firefighters, hospital ward, building site, school classroom....

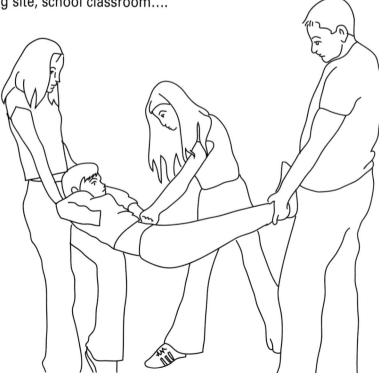

ICT

Word Banks

Organize in pairs. Each pair is given a card with a computer term on it. They then mime the term and other pairs guess what it is.

Walk Through

The class circles round the hall. Every now and again you freeze frame and say a computer term and they mime the computer term or mimic it before moving on. To start with choose easy terms and demonstrate for them. Sequence them in turn so that the links are learned.

Routines

Organize in small groups. Have each group choose a routine which involves ICT. For example starting up the machine. Have them construct a mime. The others guess what the routine is.

Do's and Don'ts

Organize in small groups. Each group then mimes some do's and don'ts when working with computers. The others guess what the do's and don'ts are.

English

Alphabet Games

Give each child a letter of the alphabet on a laminated card. Mix the children up. Quick as possible they organize themselves into the letters in the order of the alphabet.

Touch a Vowel

Mix the children up. Quick as possible they find a vowel and touch the vowel. How many are there?

Spell It

Organize the children sitting in a circle. Say a word and the letters of the word come out and spell it. Do the same for keywords. Do the same for children's names. Now get ambitious: What is the longest word we can spell? What is the funniest? What is the strangest? What is the word with the most vowels?

Active Punctuation

Choose a series of gestures to accompany speech marks and punctuation. Teach the class the gestures. Read them a section from a story and pause when a punctuation or speech mark is needed. Now together do the gesture before carrying on.

Organize the children in groups. Give each group letters of the alphabet and punctuation marks on laminated cards. Read them a section from a story and pause when a punctuation mark is needed. Each group agrees on what sort of punctuation and the person holding the card stands up.

Science

Growth and Development

Using the body to represent the life cycle or development stages of plants or animals can prompt really good questions. Laminated keywords can be used to help identify each successive development stage. Use large free spaces to work in for easy movement and so that children can get a clear view of what's happening.

Push and Pull

In pairs set up push and pull movements by holding hands. What helps and what hinders? What objects might be easy to push and what would be difficult? Why? Pull your partner across the floor gently by holding them under their arms and moving backwards? What slows you down? Would it be easier if you placed a pillow under their feet? What surfaces are easiest to pull an object across? Which are most difficult? Why?

Electrical Circuits and Conductors

Mark out an electrical circuit on the floor of the hall using rope. Have laminated cards for resistors, circuit breakers, bulbs and diodes. Have circuits in parallel and in series. Walk members of the class around the circuit and ask them to say what happens at each card.

Geography

Congestion!

Should the High Street be closed to traffic? Why? Is it congested? What is congestion? In the hall the class roams freely then we place two lengths of rope on the floor in parallel. The ropes represent the narrow High Street and the class have to roam within the ropes. What is the difference? Now try it with two streams of traffic and space for pedestrians. Allocate the roles. Note the differences. Try calming measures so that traffic has to take it in turns to go. Have observers note all the effects.

Where do we spend our time?

Using children in pairs in a large space create mimes of the different things they might do in their spare time. Others guess what it is the pairs are doing.

History

Use a time line to represent the key events in Britain since 1948 . Each child represents an event in sequence. They stand or sit in a line and step forward in sequence, using mime and gesture they demonstrate the event.

In role describe through words and movement some of the differences in the lives of rich and poor people in Tudor times.

Vox pop. Roving reporters are set up with children from the Second World War in the hall. Some children have stayed at home, some have been sent to the country or abroad. Each tells their story to the roving reporters.

Music

Exploring pulse and rhythm. Copy and practise tapping, clapping and stamping to different rhythms. Try clapping the rhythm of the numbers or the days of the week or the months of the year.

The brain-break exercises

Writers

The Principle

Brain breaks for handwriting help children rehearse the shapes of letters and words in advance of writing them on the page.

Teaching Tips

1 Use the handpen. The handpen is where the hands are clasped together as in prayer to form a 'pen'. This ensures that shaping letters is a cross lateral activity.

2 As you practise get littler and littler with the movements.

3 Complete brain breaks for handwriting before handwriting practice. Use music to help develop a steady rhythm.

Benefits to Children

1 It is a 'safe' way to practise writing and words.

2 It helps children remember the shapes of letters and of words.

3 Makes writing part of a fun activity.

Hands Together

Trace circles in the air with two hands held together. Follow your hand movements with your eyes only. Keep your head still. Keep your lips and teeth together.

Trace the number 8 in the air with two hands held together. Follow your hand movements with your eyes only. Keep your head still. Keep your lips and teeth together.

Trace the number 8 on its side in the air with two hands held together. Follow your hand movements with your eyes only. Keep your head still. Keep your lips and teeth together.

Trace a drawing of your house in the air with two hands held together. Follow your hand movements with your eyes only. Keep your head still. Keep your lips and teeth together.

Double Bubble

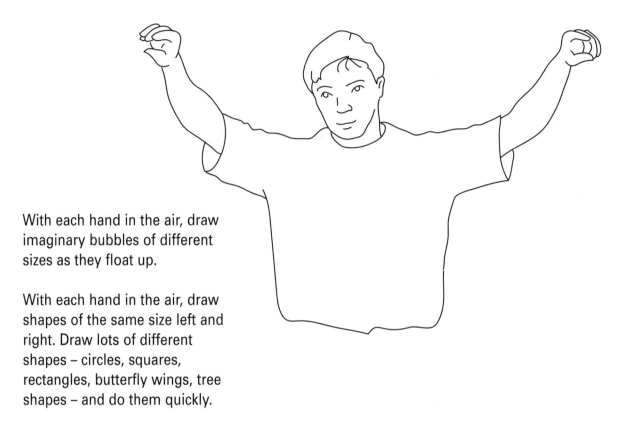

With each hand in the air, draw imaginary bubbles of different sizes as they float up.

With each hand in the air, draw shapes of the same size left and right. Draw lots of different shapes – circles, squares, rectangles, butterfly wings, tree shapes – and do them quickly.

With each hand in the air, draw letters of the alphabet of the same size left and right. Draw lots of different letters and do them quickly. Now do the same with numbers. Try doing different letters or numbers at the same time. Is it easy?

The brain-break exercises

Readers

The Principle

Brain breaks for literacy help children rehearse, explore and have fun with the shapes of letters, words and punctuation.

Teaching Tips

1 Use the handpen. The handpen is where the hands are clasped together as in prayer to form a 'pen'. This ensures that shaping letters is a cross lateral activity.

2 Build from the basics of letter shapes.

3 Reinforce with suitable visuals and with compatible paper and pencil activities.

Benefits to Children

1 It is a 'safe' way to practise writing and words.

2 It helps children remember the shapes of letters, words and punctuation.

3 Makes writing part of a fun activity.

Register Write

Everyone stands and as each name is called the class write the name in the air with their hand-pen. The person whose name has been called sits down. Each day start at a different point in your register.

Right Write

Write the keywords from the lesson in the air with one hand.

Write the keywords from the lesson in the air with two hands held together.

Write the keywords from the lesson in the air with your nose.

Write the keywords from the lesson in the air with your right ear.

Right Write (cont)

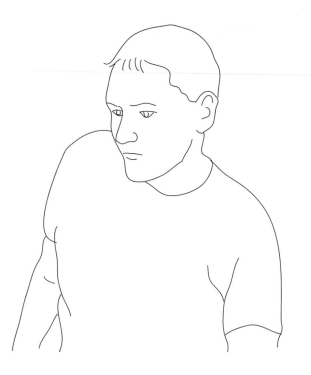

Write the keywords
from the lesson in the
air with your left ear.

Try all of the above with your eyes closed.

Try all of the above with your eyes closed and saying the letters of the
keyword to yourself as you go.

Write the keywords from the
lesson on your partner's back,
and see if they can guess
what you wrote.

Right Write (cont)

Write out letters in the air and say their names and sounds.

Write the alphabet in the air as fast as you can,
or do it all together while singing an alphabet song.

Stand on one leg while you
write the alphabet in the air.

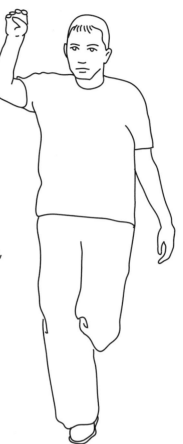

Write your name in the air – write it big, write it small, backwards,
forwards and with left hand and right hand, then with both.

Paper Right Write

Write your name on a piece of paper using both hands
and two pencils. Start in the centre and work in mirror image.

Paired Right Write

Stand opposite a partner and place your palms against your partners palms, then make the
letters of the alphabet together in the air.

Ask the teacher to
practise 'teacher says'
with you. The teacher
makes a movement and
you copy it. If the teacher
says 'do this', you do it. If
the teacher says 'do that',
you don't do it! Make sure
you listen carefully.

65

The brain-break exercises

Counters

The Principle

Brain breaks for numeracy help children rehearse, explore and have fun with patterns of number, with addition, subtraction, division and multiplication. It also helps them explore and understand different sorts of shapes.

Teaching Tips

1 Use the handpen. The handpen is where the hands are clasped together as in prayer to form a 'pen'. This ensures that shaping letters is a cross-lateral activity.

2 Start with simple number shapes.

3 Reinforce with suitable visuals and with compatible paper and pencil activities.

Benefits to Children

1 It is a 'safe' way to use numbers.

2 It helps children remember the shapes of numbers and the mechanics of the four rules of number.

3 Makes numbers enjoyable.

Number Up

Write a sum in the air, copying the teacher. Then write the answer as large as you can!

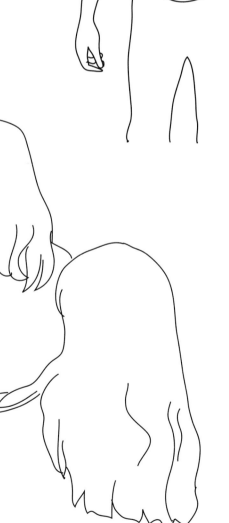

Write a sum on your partner's back. Get him to write the answer on yours. Was he right?

Number Up (cont)

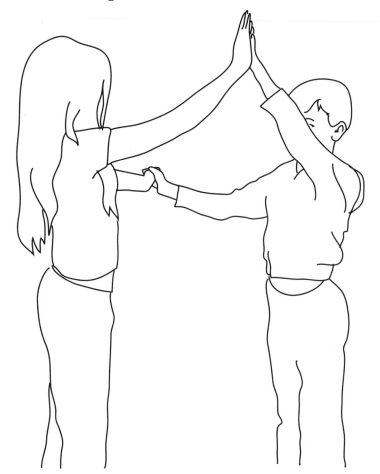

Copy a sum from the board onto your partner's back. Make sure that he can't see the board. See if he can work out the answer. Then swap.

Write the numbers in the air as you sing along to a multiplication tables song.

With a partner, make numbers with your bodies. Work your way from 1 to 10.

Number line

As a class stand in a line and shout out your number in turn. As you say your number step forward then back. Now do all the even numbers. Now do all the odd numbers. Now all the numbers which divide by 3. Now all the even numbers, numbers which divide by 3 and which have a 3 in them. Can you do it?

As a class stand in a line and shout out your number in turn. This time start with -10 and finish with +10. How many of you are there? Now practice multiplication and division. Following your teacher's directions, jump back and forth to represent multiplication or division.

Shape Up

Stand opposite a partner and place your palms against your partners palms, then make big sweeping shapes together in the air.

Swap sides and do it again. What happens?

Make 2D shapes with your body – a square, circle, rectangle, octagon.

Make 3D shapes with a partner – a cube, sphere, cylinder.

Angle Up

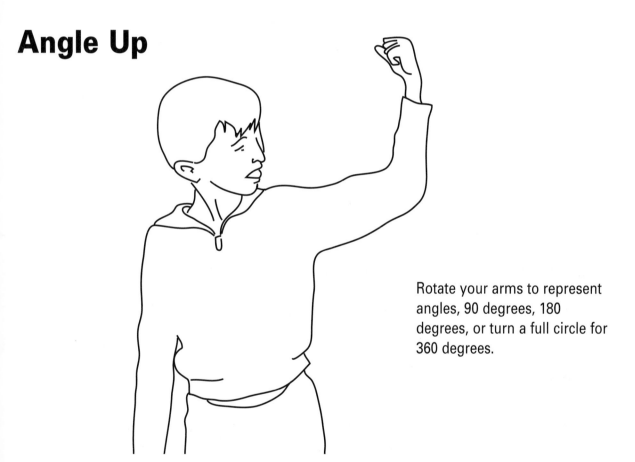

Rotate your arms to represent angles, 90 degrees, 180 degrees, or turn a full circle for 360 degrees.

Time Up

Rotate your arms to represent the time. Ask your partner to guess what time it is. Don't cheat!

The brain-break exercises

Trackers

The Principle

Eye Trackers help the child improve eye movement control. Many reading problems have their source in poor eye tracking. These activities are designed to help improve eye tracking.

Teaching Tips

1 If a child has an eye tracking problem get specialist help first; liaise with the parents.

2 Stop if the activity proves too uncomfortable or tiring for the child. Gradually build up over time.

3 Safety first when moving around. Start with easier desk-based activities.

Benefits to Children

1 It can help improve control of eye movements, particularly tracking and focus.

2 It may, as a consequence of improved control of eye movements, help with reading and writing.

3 It is safe and non-threatening.

Eyes Alive

Play eyes north, south, east and west. Without moving your head move your eyes up for north, down for south, right for west and left for east. Do it slowly at first then try it more quickly. Get your teacher to call out the directions and you move your eyes as quickly as possible.

Try eyes north, south, east and west with your eyelids closed. Can you do it? Is it easy? How would I know you had done it?

Choose three different points on the wall of the classroom. Think of them as A, B and C. Without moving your head look at each point for one second only in sequence. Now look at each point for one second only in the sequence B, A, C. Now try C, A, B. Now add another point D. Try A, D, B, C. Do it several times then change.

Wandering Eyes

With a pencil held between your finger and thumb like a wand write your name in the air with your arm outstretched. Don't move your head but watch the tip of the pencil with your eyes. Keep your head still. Watch carefully. Try it with different words including long words.

Face a partner so you can't touch each other and draw their outline in the air with two hands held together. Follow your hand movements with your eyes only. Keep your head still. Keep your lips and teeth together.

Eye Walks

In pairs,

It is possible to exercise the eyes by combining body movements with a fixed stare. Moving the body, keep the eyes still. Movements include rolling the head from side to side while focusing on a single point on the wall, or gently turning the upper body whilst focusing on a single point, or walking around an object while focusing on the object. The process is to get the eyes moving more smoothly and more often and practise tracking movements left and right, right and left.

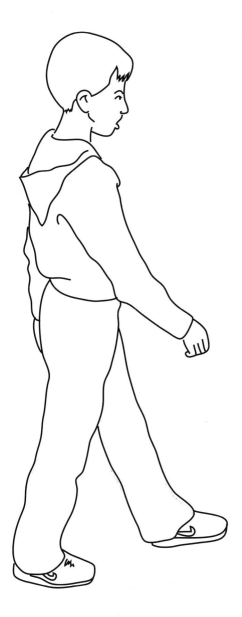

Your brain breaks may benefit from using simple apparatus. You should collect together bits and pieces to intergrate into the activities. Here are some items to get your collection started.

Large foam hands such as those you see at football matches

Plastic blow up bananas, cod, hammers, hats – again of the sort seen at football matches

Glove puppets

Koosh balls

Bean bags

Rope of various lengths to mark out shapes on the floor

Skipping ropes

Beach ball

Birthing balls

Laminated cards with letters of the alphabet in lower case for use in alphabet games

Wobble board

Skateboard

Hoops

Cones

Flags

Musical instruments

Dolls

Alphabet Soup

A	**B**	**C**	**D**	**E**
r	l	t	t	r

F	**G**	**H**	**I**	**J**
l	l	t	r	t

K	**L**	**M**	**N**	**O**
t	r	l	t	l

P	**Q**	**R**	**S**	**T**
r	t	r	l	r

U	**V**	**W**	**X**	**Y**
r	t	l	t	r

Z
t

Alphabet Duck Soup

A	B	C	D	E
r	l	t	du	r

F	G	H	I	J
l	du	t	r	t

K	L	M	N	O
t	r	l	du	l

P	Q	R	S	T
r	t	du	l	r

U	V	W	X	Y
r	t	du	du	r

Z
t

Alphabet Animal Soup

A	**B**	**C**	**D**	**E**
r	l	t	bird	r

F	**G**	**H**	**I**	**J**
l	elephant	t	r	t

K	**L**	**M**	**N**	**O**
t	r	l	horse	l

P	**Q**	**R**	**S**	**T**
r	t	horse	l	r

U	**V**	**W**	**X**	**Y**
r	t	elephant	bird	r

Z
t

www.

www.alite.co.uk — the author's site

www.kinesiology.net — an academic network for muscle testing

www.subtlenergy.com — commercial site on allergy testing

www.braingym.com — Edu-Kinesthetics Inc website

www.pesoftware.com/resources/movelearn.html — the relationship between physical activity and cognitive learning

www.brainconnection.com — the brain and learning

www.ufa.org.uk — University of the First Age

www.luckyduck.co.uk — UK publisher specializing in self-esteem products and suppliers of Write Dance

http://www.allianceforchildhood.net/ — Alliance for Childhood

http://www.nauticom.net — early years and brain-based learning

http://www.cdipage.com — the Child Development Institute

http://www.ich.ucl.ac.uk/ — Institute of Child health

http://www.hea.org.uk — Health Education Authority

http://www.nct-online.org — National Childbirth Trust

http://www.brain.com — brain com site

http://www.6seconds.org/ — Emotional Intelligence Network

http://www.bottledwater.org. — International bottled water association

http://www.british-sleep-society.org.uk/ — British Sleep Society

http://www.lboro.ac.uk	Sleep research laboratory Loughborough
http://www.ldresources.com	Learning Disabilities Resources is a US online resource site
http://www.ldonline.org	Overview of Learning Disabilities
http://www.pavilion.co.uk/add/english.html	ADD links
http://www.web-tv.co.uk/addnet.html	ADD net
http://www.bda-dyslexia.org.uk/	British Dyslexia Association
http://www.interdys.org/	The International Dyslexia Association Website
http://www.biausa.org/	Brain Injury Association
http://www.stroke.org.uk/	The Stroke Association
http://www.dyspraxiafoundation.org.uk	The Dyspraxia Foundation
http://www.nagcbritain.org.uk	National Association for Gifted Children
http://www.giftedl.uconn.edu/	US National Research Centre for Gifted and Talented
http://www.cec.sped.org	US Council for Exceptional Children
http://www.edwebproject.org/edref.mi.intro.html	Multiple intelligences site
http://www.mindinst.org/	MIND Institute Research into the Mozart Effect and Education
http://www.mri.ac.uk/	UK based music research centre
http://www.srpmme.org.uk	Society for Research in Psychology of Music and Music Education

Ten Good Books

1   Jensen, Eric *Learning with the Body in Mind, 2000*. The Brain Store, San Diego

2   Dennison, Paul and Dennison Gail, 1989. *Brain Gym: Teacher's Edition*, Ventura Ca, Edu-Kinesthetics, Inc

3   Hannaford, Carla, *Smart Moves*, 1995, Arlington, Va, Great Ocean Publishing

4   Smith, Alistair, *The Brain's Behind It*, 2002, Stafford, UK, Network Educational Press

5   Oussoren Voors, 2002, *Write Dance: A progressive music and movement programme for the development of pre-writing and writing skills in children*, Lucky Duck Publishing

6   Smith, Alistair and Call, Nicola, *The ALPS Approach*, 1999, Stafford, UK, Network Educational Press

7   Smith, Alistair and Call, Nicola, *The ALPS Approach Resource Book*, 2000, Stafford, UK, Network Educational Press

8   Buzan, Tony. *Head Strong: How to get Physically and Mentally Fit*, 2001, Thorsons, London

9   Howard, Pierce, J. *The Owner's Manual for the Brain*, 1996, Nard Press, Texas

10 Portwood, Madeleine., *Developmental Dyspraxia: Identification and Intervention*, 2nd edn, David Fulton Publishing London 1999